American Indian Weaving

Brenda Parkes

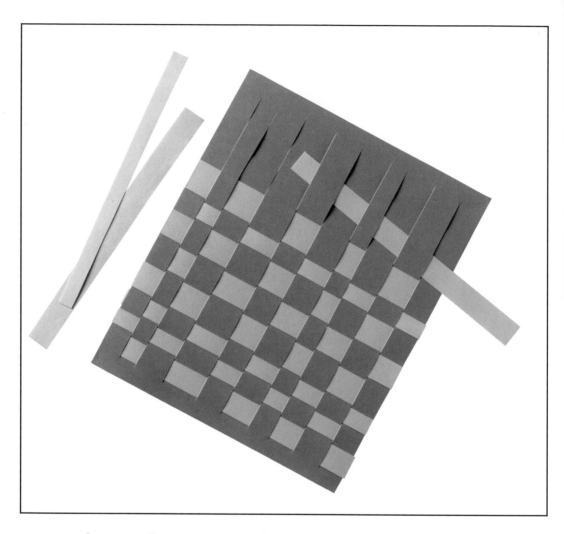

This shows what weaving is.
You can weave
placemats like this one.

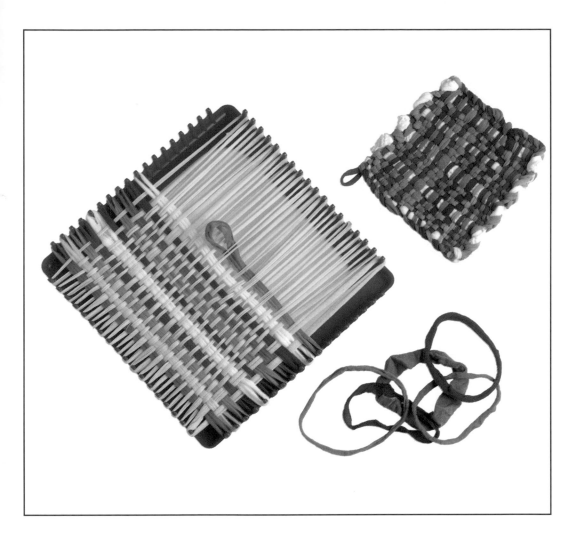

You can weave
potholders like these, too.
In and out, over and under.

Long ago, American Indian weavers
made wonderful things
for people to use.

The Navajo people
wove warm blankets.
Their beautiful blankets
were made of wool.

The Navajo weavers wove blankets
on a loom like this.
In and out, over and under.

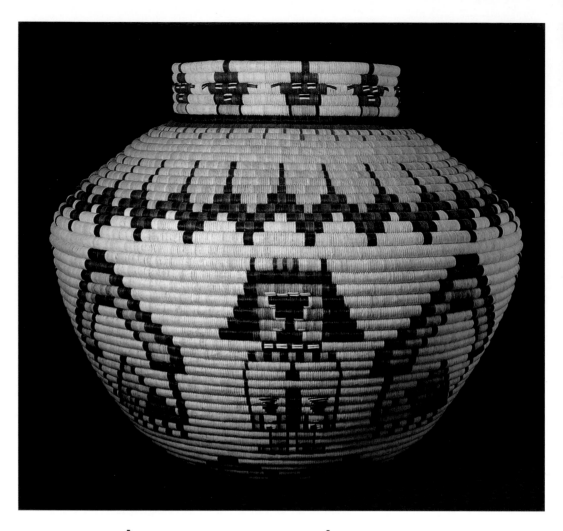

The Hopi people
wove strong baskets.

They made their baskets
from parts of plants.

The Pomo weavers
wove baskets, too.
They used
beads and feathers
to decorate their baskets.

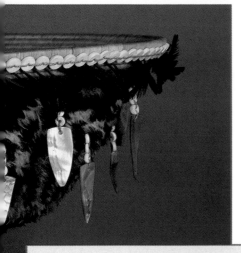

They made baskets
of different shapes
and sizes.

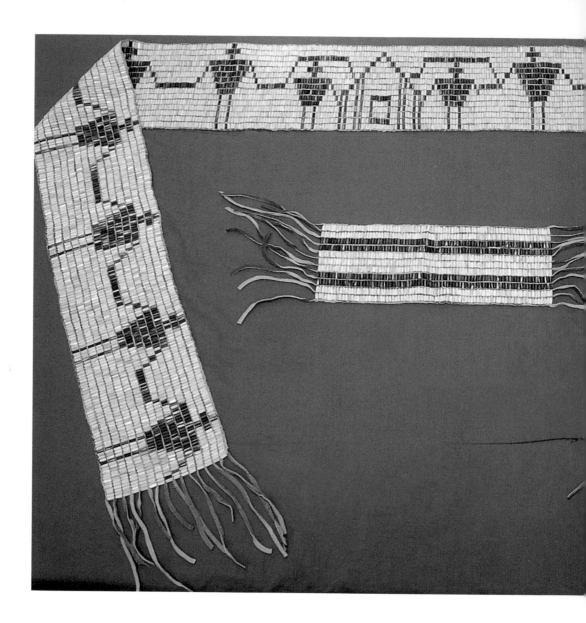

The Iroquois people wove wampum belts. The belts were made with strings of purple and white beads.

American Indian weavers
have always woven
pictures and patterns.

Even today, American Indians weave beautiful things.